COMMON ENEMY

THE COMMON BATTLE FOR ALL PUBLIC SERVANTS

ISRAEL RODRIGUEZ

Trilogy Christian Publishers

A Wholly Owned Subsidary of Trinity Broadcasting Network

2442 Michelle Drive

Tustin, CA 92780

For information, address Trilogy Christian Publishing

Rights Department, 2442 Michelle Drive, Tustin, Ca 92780.

Trilogy Christian Publishing/ TBN and colophon are trademarks of Trinity Broadcasting Network.

For information about special discounts for bulk purchases, please contact Trilogy Christian Publishing.

Manufactured in the United States of America

10 9 8 7 6 5 4 3 2 1

Library of Congress Cataloging-in-Publication Data is available.

ISBN 878-1-68556-308-0

ISBN 978-1-68556-309-7 (ebook)

DEDICATION

This book is dedicated to all the men and women who have committed their lives to serving others. For the first responders who are just beginning on the front lines, to those who have completed their assignment, your devotion to serve and protect will never go unnoticed.

FOREWORD

Prayer for the person holding the book:

Heavenly Father, I pray that you bless the person holding this book. That it speaks directly to any problem they may be facing. That it cast out anything that may come against them, and that if they have gone through any hardship, they recognize this book to be the link to you. The link that will restore them and set them free. I pray if anyone does not know anything about becoming a believer in you or how to pray, I pray this book to be the bridge in that gap Lord. In Jesus name, Amen.

PREFACE

While working in law enforcement and serving in ministry, the two have become so interconnected its uncanny. It's ironic to think living a life so closely blended between the two would allow you to see things so differently. Yet somehow, you become so inspired by seeing where life's real problems lie and how to contribute toward a solution. As times change and working in public service gets harder for many, I believe God has put it on my heart to provide a resource and support system for those who serve on the front line. This book was originally planned to be two separate books. One being a resources guide and the second being a prayer book to provide a tangible resource for first responders. Thanks to the partners at TBN, these books have been combined to provide a resources guide and prayer book to have the tools directly following the vital information learned to be able to put the protection into action. This book also serves as a ministry launch tool for *Stable Ministries*. A ministry designed to provide support in several aspects for first responders and their families. I ask as you navigate this book, you keep an open mind, a receptive heart and a willing spirit.

ACKNOWLEDGMENTS

To God be the glory for the opportunity to share this book. This book was made possible in part by the following Stable Ministries partners. Larry & Diana Rodriguez and my beautiful wife Audrey Rodriguez. Reverend Jeffrey and Maria Sutton with Living Word Family Ministries. Pastor Jeremy Sullivan with Faith Community Church Las Cruces. Ruben Herrera with Herrera Reality LLC. Vince Vaccaro with Lorenzo's Italian Restaurant. Quality Life Services, Sandy Hill, Felipe Hernandez and Leslie Molina. A big thank you to the Triumphantlife Church family who support us every week as our home church.

INTRODUCTION

This book is for the first responder. The hospital emergency room staff, the paramedic, emergency medical technician, firefighter, correctional officer, and anyone who wears a uniform of any type of law enforcement. All the above-mentioned careers face a common enemy in this world. However, that enemy is not the gangbanger hustling drugs down the street. It is not the bank robber that causes panic, or the drunk person who puts up a fight at the bar. It is the enemy that causes stress, anxiety, and depression at home. It's what causes many great first responders to lose their jobs or make poor decisions. It is the Common Enemy of wrongdoing. Working in the field, in accountability, and above all else, ministry, I have seen all too many times the personal issues that front-line workers face. But it's the unspoken issues that are the consistent fight that sometimes causes people to fall. Sometimes, it is through no fault of the individual, while other times it is a specific decision to do wrong that causes many to stumble out of public service.

This book is designed to acknowledge that no one person is alone in the internal battles they face. Historically, (and sometimes generationally) there are reoccurring issues first responders face for doing the jobs they do. My prayer is that you read this book with an open mind and an open heart. To self-evaluate and ask yourself what decisions you are making and what attack is trying to bring you down in life. Whether it be spiritually, physically, or financially, the goal for a first responder is to go home safe every day. However, I believe the second most important rule is to go home sane and strong. If you are wanting a change in your life and are willing to make that change after a self-reflection, then this book is for you. Remember, you are not alone in facing this common enemy. Nor do you have to go through this career alone. If you find yourself right amid some of these conflicts, know that you also do not have to restore yourself alone.

It is difficult for first responders to seek help. However, if you do not seek to fix a problem, you will endure it until you reach a breaking point. Read through, then reach out, then believe within, and lastly, Grow! Grow in faith and enjoy your life. Know that what you did when the ride is over, and all is said and done was well worth it. That the way you did everything was honorable and with integrity. You will also find in this book a resource guide in the form of a months' worth of prayers. 30 prayers to pray before every shift to keep you accountable, thinking and protected as you go into the field to serve others. I pray that this book will bless you. May God protect you, move in your life, keep you and your family happy. May you from the moment you start and complete this book, live an enjoyable, safe and fulfilled life. In Jesus' name, Amen.

TABLE OF CONTENTS

WHAT WE FACE ON THE FRONT LINE!

If you work in any public service line of work, some struggles are encountered on the daily. Whether it be with the very people we serve or coworkers, we know that it doesn't take much to ruin a day when we are already pouring out so much. But would you believe that there is a common enemy we all face working in public service? I am not talking about anything mystical or magical. I truly am talking about spiritual warfare that exists because the job you do is naturally Christ-like. You working as a first responder, a paramedic, a law enforcement officer, a veteran, an emergency room staff member, you have served others and operate in an area of life where people rely on you. With this knowledge, it makes sense that if anyone can pull you down from what you do, they will try to because it would allow for one less person doing good in this world.

Often, we would believe that someone else is trying to make us fall. That there is a demon inside of someone trying to come against us. But we tend to overlook the decisions and the gradual attacks in our hearts and minds that cause ourselves to stumble. I have seen many great first responders fall because of self-inflicted decisions inside and outside their professions that cost them their entire careers. For some, it cost them their livelihood. Some of these decisions could be as little as laziness or as significant as criminal conduct and policy violations. It's time we are honest with ourselves and the realm we work in. We must understand the common enemies that bring public servants and first responders down. Below are the most common, unspoken, reoccurring issues we face in these professions. We need to identify these areas and face them head-on if we want to live an enjoyable life.

- Alcohol
- Drugs
- Sex
- Affairs
- Promiscuity
- Post-Traumatic Stress Disorder
- Ego-Narcissism
- Laziness – Negligence
- Attitude
- Depression
- Domestic Violence

The decisions surrounding these issues vary by situation. Some people start with childhood trauma and "generational curses" that make them go into their profession. They felt the need to be the change in the world, but never were able to get rid of their baggage before going into their line of work. While others gradually developed issues because of the work environment they were in. As the old expression goes, it is not about how it starts but rather how you finish. The only problem with that expression is, we overlook all the work and battle that is in the middle. When a runner starts a race, the setup is easy enough. You know what is about to happen, you prep, you get into position, then you start. When the runner finishes, they get to relax, slow down and reflect on the results. But the challenge is the hustle, sweat, tears, aches, and pains endured during the run that can be easily overlooked. In the same regard, all that is endured during the run may feel like it is never going to end while you are going through it.

This is exactly where I want you to be in thought as you read through this book. If you are retired, think of what chains you want to break so you can enjoy retirement without baggage from your career. If you are just starting, think of what problems you want to make sure you never have as you go through your career. For those already in or nearing retirement, think of what fight you are in and make a conscious decision now. A conscious decision that you are going to stop and change for the better.

WHAT'S OUR FAULT AND WHAT'S NOT?

It is important to understand, only one of these issues can potentially be a desire. But my prayer is that no one is truly that self-centered to the point that they seek to embrace whatever their internal conflicts are. Make sure you are not that person that is accepting of their ego while dealing with these issues. A person like that would be narcissistic and want to identify that before even attempting to change for the better. If you cannot admit you have an issue to start, you will always have trouble.

However, a lot of the issues such as depression, attitude, alcoholism, and domestic violence can be directly connected to job-related stress. Many people have gone through the profession and never had issues until working as a first responder. This is important to identify all that you suffer from and what you never want to deal with while in your career. In the previous chapter, it was mentioned for some, childhood trauma led to the motivation for the career. Some examples are growing up in a low-income environment or enduring something that a stranger put you through. It drove you to want to become a difference-maker for your community so that it would not happen to someone else.

But often, we look over the fact that placing someone in an environment so toxic for so long could result in revictimized feelings. There have been records across the nation of first responders finding themselves working so closely in the area that scared them, they lose sight of why they are there. They become distracted or tempted by the comfortability of work, slowly and sometimes unknown to the individual, they fall into the temptation of the enemy. A hospital worker getting comfortable with the access he or she has to the prescriptions. Possibly, the staff conducting medical practices outside the facility such as IV's for drunk friends. The firefighter becoming too heroic to realize the continuous white night syndrome he enjoys when assisting a woman. The power and authority going straight to the head of the cop or military person. If it starts to feel like these topics are right up in your backyard, that's good.

It is time we break through the fourth wall of what truly goes on behind the scenes and what real people are dealing with. However, those same three examples could be applied to someone who never suffered childhood trauma. The job itself could create a person to become something they never were. This is the part I pray for you to discover and keep in the back of your mind for the rest of your career. You must make the decision that you will identify when you start to feel tempted and you will shut it off as soon as you even think, smell, or see what you know could be a problem for your future. Some refer to it as a shield or trigger guard, others will refer to it as a fence, whatever fits for your analogy. Just know you should stop it as soon as you know it could lead down a path of destruction. Never forget, you will have to revisit this mindset to stop bad decisions as you go through your entire career.

It is human nature to test the waters to see how far you will go with something. Just as a child will continue to stretch how far they can go with their parents; I am sure everyone has seen how long they can go with stretching freedom at work. Whenever you feel that something is not being fair, there is nothing wrong with speaking up. No one can get upset at you for voicing what you feel is right for the circumstances you are surrounded by. On the flip side of that, I would also ask myself, "Is this for my gain?" If you simply are stretching practices so you can do something that a member of the public would question your integrity on, do you think it's the right thing to do?

WHO ASKS FOR HELP? WHY SHOULD YOU?

It is very difficult for first responders to seek help in their career field. No one wants to admit to having issues or appear as they are unfit to perform the job they enjoy. There are several examples of this that happen all around us that we become oblivious to. You don't think your coworker is drinking too much, you don't want to believe your supervisor is a domestic abuser or you don't want to admit you are having marital issues. Until something happens, then the other old phrase comes to rise, "I never would have guessed they did that!"

There have been many first responders who have gone to the company-provided counselor or psychologist to seek help for their issues. Only for the counselor to check the boxes off that they were fine and good to go back to work. Sometimes the help that is recommended would have to be on your own time and money and creates another hurdle in seeking help. All when you only developed your problem because of doing your very best for the place you thought you wanted to give your life for. The answer for who asks for help is simple, everyone should. This is the day in age where if you need help, point blank, you need to ask. Stop pretending like it's wrong or makes you less of a person to ask for something. I'll never forget hearing brother Keith Moore say, "I have got more going on in my life than to worry about what's going on in your head about me." That phrase marked me. It challenged me to always remind myself that no matter what people think of me, it doesn't matter. I still must go through life and cannot base life decisions on the way other people think.

The best analogy I can think of to put this into practice, is the man facing a terminal illness who does not want to go to the hospital because he is afraid, he will look weak. When the fact of the matter is that decision itself could cost him his life, and the fact that he did not want to look weak would not even be a thought in someone's mind. Bottom line, you need help, get help. That also answers the question of why you should. If you neglect a health concern in your body, there is a good chance it could get worse. The principle is the same in life, if you neglect a bad habit, it could become worse. Some coworkers like to socially drink after work, but a couple of times one is too intoxicated to walk out on his own. He gets a ride and makes it home with no issues. No harm no foul, right? If we do not see any issues with that from the start, we are not seeing correctly.

Fifteen years into playing softball and drinking on the prison softball team, never had any issues. Until one day it costs you a career or worse, someone's life. These issues did not just go from zero to one hundred overnight. They all had to start somewhere. If you find yourself having trouble asking yourself why you should ask for help, ask someone else who could tell you honestly. There have been many cases of people over the years who were initially upset at their best friends and family because they sought out help for the person with the problem. However, when it was all said and done, they were glad they did. Below you will find a cheat sheet to check yourself and see if you are falling into any of the categories.

- Do you drink every day? Do you drink because of work?
- Are you engaging in an affair? Are you cheating on your significant other?
- Do you take items from work, and no one knows about them?
- Do you find ways to get out of work? Do you simply not do it because the policy doesn't say you can't?
- Do you get angry quickly or frequently? Do you yell sporadically and clench your fists? Do you take it out on your family?
- Do you spend too much time at work?
- Do you only hang out with other coworkers in the same profession as you?
- Do you gossip and spread rumors?
- Do you need help with anything and why?

FAITH TO MAKE IT THROUGH THE CAREER, FAITH TO ENJOY RETIREMENT!

This book is meant for not only those currently working as a first responder but for those who have already finished their ride and are enjoying retirement. There are a lot of first responders who devote their lives to serving others and when it is all said and done, they pass away from some sort of untimely issue. Cancer, car accident, suicide. Just because you already ran your race, doesn't mean you cannot still treat your body.

For example, if you are retired and suffer from depression or PTSD, it is never too late to seek help for those issues. In my opinion, everyone who has served their part in this fight of life deserves to rest at the end of the road. For those who are just getting into their careers or still in, we should look at the finish line of the career with the same paradise mentality. We want to retire without issues or suffering anything to live along with life. However, 20-30 years of a career is a lot of time and should not just pass us by without living every moment to the fullest. Yes, 20 years can seem like just yesterday to some. But if you enjoy every minute of every single one and not just count them down, you won't pass over a large chunk of your life.

You may have noticed I haven't used a lot of scripture thus far; it is for a reason. Everything that has already been mentioned believe it or not falls in line with what the bible says about your life and what is promised for you. This chapter is where the faith meets the fight. The bible defines faith as the substance of things hoped for and the evidence of things not seen. It's already been mentioned, serving others, and having the desire to help others is exactly a quality of what Jesus was sent to this world to do.

Whether you believe in God or not, the truth is the devil does not like anything that even remotely resembles Jesus Christ. That's why even though you may not be a believer of the faith, the enemy wants people to suffer and go through hardships. That is why your decision to serve others sometimes has you questioning why you are doing what you are doing or why you are facing what you are facing. Why did my parents pass away, why did I get fired, why did I do that? Until you realize there are other spiritual forces at work on this earth, you'll never understand how to live your life.

I heard it said once, you will never find a purpose until you are serving God. That stands true today more than it ever did. Drug dealers are turning their life around in one day because they find faith. They go from 24-hour drug dealers to never looking at another narcotic again. Simply because they found a God who forgives them and wants to see them go on the right path. The same can be said for many who have been incarcerated and released with a new mission in life to help others not make the same mistakes they did. My question of faith to you is if these people who don't work as the first responder can turn their life around for the better. Why can't you? There is no good reason you cannot do what you do as a first responder and still want to have a long-blessed life with purpose in it.

WHY WE DO
WHAT WE DO

I'll never forget a retired captain once told me, the real criminals are the ones who manipulate the badge or oath. It was another quote that marked me. Holding accountability and integrity is nothing to be ashamed about. The stigma towards any branch of enforcement these days has gotten worse and worse. Do you want the truth of it though? The real issue of lack of trust in law enforcement does not come from the protests and high-profile cases that make people label all first responders as bad.

The real lack of trust is because the men and women in our community see you when you are outside of work. They see you trying to be the difference-maker in taking DWI's off the street but drink to the point of blackout every Friday, Saturday, and Sunday night. They see you trying to talk to people who have domestic issues like they are causing an inconvenience to everyone in the neighborhood. Yet they see you and your spouse arguing and cheating on each other all the time. They know you follow policies at work on what to do but hear you bragging about how you beat someone up. These are the same stories that get passed around from your family and friends to the other members of the public that eventually get back to you.

If there is nothing else you take from this chapter, know that lack of trust in this profession has grown not necessarily because of perception, rather through observation. Now as a disclaimer, this is not the same in every area across the nation. But it is a core issue in a lot of organizations. As you involve more coworkers or begin to cover for each other simply because you can, makes for a reasonable argument for anyone to ask how they can trust you.

These professions are already defined by integrity, professionalism and respect. Who you are inside and outside of work only adds or subtracts from it. When people can correlate an honorable person interchangeably with an honorable profession, it makes for a blissful feeling for everyone involved. You never have to worry about someone questioning your character, someone questioning the integrity of the organization. You can stand boldly and confidently in what you stand for and what you represent. Now add a faith element in there, now you are living with eternal purpose now.

I'd rather spend my time making a difference in my church raising students to stay off the street and make a difference in their lives. While also exercising my faith by gaining more knowledge about what life is truly about.

Why I am here on this earth and what is promised for me by God. I'll be honest, living life in that manner in this profession does bring a lot of persecution. You need to make another heart-centered decision that you won't be moved by other people's opinions of you.

People won't like the fact that you have changed, that you do not do the same things they do. You won't test the waters anymore as they do. Another great quote, a drowning man always tries to pull some one down with them. People will judge you and call you a hypocrite. The best way to negate all of that is found once again in scripture. Continue to live your life a living sacrifice, holy and acceptable to the Lord. Meaning, if you are going to commit to living a life of integrity in your line of work. You are either all in or you are not. If you are going to start fulfilling your purpose by getting involved in church or finding faith, then you need to live by what it teaches and what it says. Otherwise, you will be a hypocrite. It is not easy to be the person that lives a certain way because of the way they believe. But the best part is you know what you stand for, and people identify you with that.

SUPPORT STRUCTURES AND RESOURCES

If you have ever made a costly mistake at work (I.E. got arrested and lost your job, made an immoral decision that cost you your job) there is no reason you cannot be restored from that. Who you are is not who you were from that anymore, but you have to take that to heart. You have got to learn from your mistakes and not stress over them. We only get one life on this earth, it's cliche but so true. One chance to enjoy the actual feel of joy and happiness in the fleshly body. If you made a decision that causes embarrassment or backlash and cost you a lot, you can make a comeback.

The bible said as far as the east is from the west, God doesn't remember your sins. If you are willing to confess to God, I messed up and I repent. You can start a new, tough path. I won't lie to you, becoming stronger and growing not only as a person but in life is not easy. But it is the right thing to do, and it is a simple concept to understand. If you are right in the middle of an unknown circumstance where you might lose your lively hood or no longer work in the profession you devoted yourself to be in. My advice is to finish honorably and focus on your purpose for life from here. For those who never had to deal with these types of issues and are praying they never have to, I don't know about you, But I am so grateful for wisdom. God says He'll give anyone wisdom who asks of it from him. I truly believe it's something we take for granted. So, use the wisdom of learning about these topics and know you don't have to endure it to prevent it.

Therefore, I commend you for reading this book. Books are one of the best ways you can gain wisdom without having to endure something. That's the best hack of life, if you can learn about what to do for certain circumstances in life why wouldn't you take it? So, if you ever had to face it or if you get asked about it, you know what to do without ever experiencing the pain or trouble. This book is of hundreds of thousands of resources and support structures you can use to make life changes for the better. Of course, a bible believing church in your local area is my next recommendation. A lot of times, worldly counselors and doctors just are not going to understand. But when you go seeking faith-based answers for faith-based questions, you'll get attentive ears willing to help and want you to grow. In more ways than one!

If jumping into a walk with God is too much for you, start an accountability group. In this case, get a mix of people who share the same values of change to meet on the weekly and merely hang out and discuss these topics. It is therapeutic and starts the process for multiple people to build the courage they need to start. Leave the beer and other items out that may hinder some people but have a barbeque or going out at night. Try and integrate coworkers and non-coworkers so there's different input. Above all else, do not just do anything. Tell yourself now, I won't have these issues, and I will do what it takes to never have them.

REMEMBER WHY THIS IS IMPORTANT!

Quite simply put, lives are on the line. Trust is on the line; our world is changing every single day. The struggles are real and sometimes unfair to those who try to do what they can to live their life right. In the past several years we have seen law enforcement ridiculed for the work they do to fight crime. Border Patrol agents have been stuck taking the criticism for decisions made beyond their control, while also dealing with issues some know nothing about. Hospital and medical staff have been judged for the lifesaving measures they have chosen to implement. Correctional officers are asked of so much yet exhausted from what they give. Firemen, working hard but many never seeing the side effects of what they suffer. Military service members, still suffering side effects from their heroic acts overseas but are often overlooked as time goes on. Never forget why these topics are important and why your life is even more important.

30 DAY PRAYERS FOR THE FIRST RESPONDER

The pages to follow were originally planned for a separate prayer book. Thanks to the partners at TBN, this book is now available as a resource tool along with the common enemy book to allow public servants to be equipped with the knowledge and faith to combat any obstacle they may face before any given shift.

1

PRAYER FOR THE JOB

Father in the Name of Jesus, I pray a spirit of protection over me and my job. I pray that I go in equipped, alert, and hungry to have a servant's heart to protect and serve those who entrust me with their lives. I pray you watch over me as I check in until I check out and that I have a joyful attitude while doing it. For I know those who will never see or know what I do today will have another day of life because of it. In Jesus name, amen.

2

PRAYER FOR FAMILY

Heavenly Father, I pray that you watch over my family as I attend work. Make sure they are protected with good health, and no weapon formed against them will prosper. As they support me for the work that I do, I pray you give them peace, health, and strength to be a part of this family that does the work of peace in this community. I pray that you would use them to be examples of how a family walks in peace and joy while they serve their community. In Jesus name, amen.

<u>3</u>

PRAYER FOR THE SUPERVISOR

Father, as I embark on my next shift, I pray that you guide my supervisor _____ (by name) in their decision making. That as they go through their shift, they would reach decisions made in the best interest of the public and the safety of me. Father, I ask that they impose your will to have everyone make it through another day in faith, peace, and joy and that they not lose sight because of power. Protect them to protect the front line. In Jesus name, amen.

4

PRAYER FOR THE DISTRACTIONS

Dear God, as I prep for another shift, I ask that you keep me from any distractions that the workplace may cause. Both work affiliated and not work affiliated. That the people who entrust me with their lives and health would not suffer for any distractions I may encounter. Allow me to focus on the job I am hired to do and to do it with a spirit of excellence until my shift is over. I know falling for distractions at work or anything that pulls me away from my work, could ruin trust in my ability to do my job. So, I ask God for your intervention in allowing me to focus. In the name of Jesus, amen.

5

PRAYER FOR PTSD

Dear God, today I pray for everything I have seen or dealt with that has stayed upon my heart and mind. Whether it be career-long or just after a traumatic event, I pray that you give me peace and the ability to not have to live with it for my life. It is by your strength that I can do this job, so I ask you to remove anything that would not allow me to walk free from the remembrance of hard times or free from peace in my day-to-day life outside of it. I WILL BE FREE OF PTSD, In Jesus' name, amen.

(1 Corinthians 2:16 KJV)

<u>6</u>

PRAYER FOR STRENGTH

Father God, today I pray that you give me a new strength to continue to work in this field. I pray that you pour out a new anointing of strength so that I may get a second breath of life to continue to walk in or after this line of work strong with energy. I pray that if I have been dwindling in my physical ability, you allow this prayer to bring light to me to continue to get back to a fitness comfortability for my work. And should I ever need it at work, your supernatural strength would intervene whenever necessary. In Jesus' name, Amen. (Isaiah 40:31 KJV)

7

PRAYER AGAINST ALCOHOL

Dear Heavenly Father, I know that as a first responder or front-line worker, many turn to alcohol to cope with several aspects of this job. I pray that I find the ability to replace that urge with you. I pray for the ability to help those who struggle with this also. For I know a beverage cannot undo physical and psychological years of public service to people. However, through you, I can find a new purpose and ability to get through every day and be an example to others on how to live a happy life free of alcohol-related problems. Many have lost careers and lives to this issue, and I pray I am not one of them. Intervene with your conviction father when I need it, In Jesus' name, amen.

8

PRAYER AGAINST LUST

Father God, I pray that I do not struggle in lust as I go through my day. As this career is affiliated with incestuous nature, I pray that I do not contribute to it father. I pray that my future or present spouse be the focus and pillar of my family, as when this career is over, I know it is them that will always be there for me. I know that too many individuals have lost creditability of trust and worse have lost careers over decisions of the flesh, may I not forget the purpose for why I am in this line of work and the example I can be by respecting those around me and allowing me and my spouse (future spouse) to be the ones to reap the benefits of a healthy marriage and family life. In Jesus' name. Amen

9

PRAYER AGAINST STRESS

Dear God, allow stress to not overtake my life. I know my job requires a lot from me. Between quick decisions, high-stress situations, emotional roller coasters, do not allow me to be overcome by stress. I know that stress can take years off of life, and I refuse to be one to allow that. Father, intervene whenever I feel stress throughout today and give me peace that I can't explain but will know it's you when I feel it. While chaos is running rapid, I will be able to think smoothly and tackle any objective I need to meet, in the name of Jesus, amen. (Philippians 4:7)

10

PRAYER AGAINST ANXIETY

Father God, I pray that I do not suffer from anxiety. That sound thought and decision-making allows me to sleep peacefully at night and allow me to function peacefully throughout the day. Coworkers cannot affect me, criminals cannot affect me, patients cannot affect me, I only operate in a realm where I hear your voice. And no matter what anyone else says, it will not have a physical bearing on me in any form. In Jesus' name, amen.

11

PRAYER AGAINST DEPRESSION

Father God, I come against any form of depression that may arise inside of me. I pray that you remove anything that does not represent you. Anything that is not of Love, Joy, Peace, Thanks, Patience, Kindness, Forgiveness. Depression is not something that you place on people, so as I go about my day and finish whatever my assignment of work is, I pray that you allow me to do it joyfully. Depression will not take years off of my life, and I will live my life with you God, to the fullest. Amen.

12

PRAYER AGAINST LAZINESS

Dear Father, I know too many good people have lost their careers due to laziness. I know that not finishing an assignment to perfection is not of you. Whether my job requires me to stay later, do more work, changes policy, or asks me to go above and beyond or simply becomes mundane. I ask that you allow me the ability to remember I am called to do this job not by choice, but because you need me here to do it the right way. I will not allow laziness to corrupt my work ethic and be what defines me, Lord. In Jesus' name, amen.

13

PRAYER FOR COWORKERS

Father God, watch over my brother and sisters in the field. Allow them to make decisions that allow us all to go home safe and sound and excited to serve another day in our respective assignments. Remove any jealousy, laziness, foul thinking, or disservice to not come into any of our hearts. Forgive the coworkers who lose sight of working as one unit. I ask you to remove pride and arrogance as well as any laziness from them Father. I ask that I not fall into any of that type of mindset while I work, and I stand in boldness for what's right. In Jesus' name, amen.

14

PRAYER FOR SPOUSE

Father God, watch over my spouse (future spouse if single) protect them in the same manner you do for me. I know being the spouse of someone on the front lines plays an equally demanding role on the person who is standing with that person. Allow them the longevity to stand with me until death does us part. For not only will their support each day get me through this career. But their support after this career will allow me to enjoy everyday life with them after this career. Protect them in their day-to-day activities as well and whatever they may be going through. In the name of Jesus, amen.

15

PRAYER FOR ANGER

Dear God, I ask that you allow me to be slow to anger. Dealing with people in this career field takes a lot of patience. I ask that you allow me to have all I need to function in this career field. Anger can result in poor decision-making and hurt necessary relationships to successfully serve and protect those who need it the most. So, I ask that any old anger, new anger, or frustrating events that occur throughout my days would be removed and be replaced with patience by you God. In Jesus' name, amen.

<u>16</u>

PRAYER FOR PROGRESSION

Father God, I pray that my career continues to be led in favor by you. Whatever that looks like to you Father, I pray your hand is upon it. Whether it be promotions, a transfer, or even a milestone achieved. I pray that you are always involved in those aspects of my career, and I never forget those blessings that come from you. I pray in Jesus' name, amen.

17

PRAYER AGAINST TEMPTATION

Father, I pray that any temptation to do wrong or corruption in my line of work be cast out by you. I know that many who operate in this world can be persuaded or manipulated into wrongdoing, and I ask that I be guided by you. That you give me the ability to know right from wrong immediately when I see it. I pray I feel your conviction when the opportunity is before me Father. And that I know that temptation is what drives the criminals of this world further and that is not me. I ask this in the name of your son, Jesus Christ, Amen.

<u>18</u>

PRAYER FOR STABILITY

Father, this career field requires a lot for one person to do in 20 to 30 years. I ask that so long as I am in this career field serving others, my ride is smooth and consistent. That although times and people change, my work ethic does not. My way of serving others does not, and my credibility does not. I want to always be reliable for those who need me and to support that way of life. I ask you to give me stability in my career and my home life so that I can reflect on how you operate in my life. In Jesus' name, amen.

19

PRAYER FOR ENDURANCE

Dear Heavenly Father, I pray that you give me supernatural endurance to do this job. I know this career will ask a lot of me (or has already asked a lot out of me.) However, I pray that I can continue everyday life with energy and excitement. That no matter how much is taken out of me, I know you have the ability to fill me right back up with enthusiasm and strength. And for that Father I thank you. In Jesus' name, amen.

<u>20</u>

PRAYER FOR UNIFICATION

Dear Father, I pray that you unify all those at my place of employment. Whether it be with contractors or those from other agencies, allow us to not lose sight of the common goal we seek to achieve. To be a peacemaker in this world, we are required to work amongst many. To be a part of an army that seeks to serve and protect life, we must work alongside many. Allow us to work as one team in one accord, united by your covering Father. Allow the prayers for our agencies to continue in our meetings. Allow your guidance and grace to be recognized amongst our agency heads' lords. And above all, allow your hand to be upon me as I am a part of this goal unification lord. In Jesus' name, amen.

21

PRAYER FOR LEADERSHIP

Father God, I know you are responsible for putting all those who are in authority. Whether I agree with it or not, I know in my heart it is for a purpose in my life. I pray for you to watch over whoever is in a position of authority over me. Father, that you will guide them correctly. But more so Father, I ask that you give me the ability to become a leader that is Christ-like. That exemplifies qualities and characteristics that Jesus did when He was here on earth. That I may be humble but bold when others look to me. In Jesus' name, amen.

22

PRAYER FOR DECISION MAKING

Father God, I know for whom much is given, much is required. I know the expectation from supervisors and the public I serve are high. I pray in the quick decisions I make; you guide me and ensure that my mind makes them according to my training and for the best possible outcome. I pray for my decisions to engage in activities outside work are made with my career and family in mind. I also add that my future is protected by the Godly decisions you would have me make. I thank you for the renewing of my mind during this time and during this prayer. In Jesus' name, Amen.

23

PRAYER FOR DOUBT

Father God, I come against any doubt that I may have regarding my public service or my decision to be in this career. Father, I also add that any doubt I have in you or belief in these prayers be cast out in the name of Jesus. To walk in your grace requires me to walk by faith. Faith means believing in your work and in what you do in your life. Let no doubt ruin my faith. In Jesus' Name, Amen.

24

PRAYER FOR BOLDNESS

Heavenly Father, I ask that you give me the boldness to stand for what is right in my life. Both in my career and my personal life. I will have the faith to speak up in my job when I know what is right. Regardless if it causes me persecution, I know you promise to protect what is right. The bible says if you are for me then who can be against me, and because it says that I know I can have the boldness to speak to those who need to hear from me what is right. Allow me to be humble and not condescending during this time as I encounter these moments of boldness Father. I thank you for allowing me to know you are with me at all times, so I never feel alone. Should I need to seek help for battles no one knows I am facing, allow me to have the boldness to ask for help. I will not be embarrassed; I will not be scared, I will not second guess what I know I need to do. In Jesus' name, amen.

<u>25</u>

PRAYER FOR RESTORATION

Dear Heavenly Father, I ask for whatever I have lost during my time in this career, you restore me. Whether it be loved ones, whether it be emotional pieces of me. Or whether it be physical losses that I have endured, I ask you to restore me to where I need to be. If I have changed because of situations in my life that I have faced, I ask you to restore me. I will not face sleepless nights, no post-traumatic stress disorder, no loss of finances, no loss of life. In Jesus' Name, amen.

<u>26</u>

PRAYER FOR THE COURAGE TO PRESS FORWARD

Father God, as I reach day twenty-six of this prayer book. I ask for the endurance to keep pressing forward in these prayers. I know whether I see it work in my life immediately or whether it takes time. I trust that you will give me spiritual endurance to keep running this race. As for my career, I pray I do not become exhausted from serving others. Your word says we are to serve others and we can pour out because you, in turn, will refill us, so I never have to feel burnt out. I pray I can press on, press forward, and will continue. In the name of Jesus, amen.

27

PRAYER FOR RETIREMENT

Father God, I know you are all-knowing. I know you know the beginning from the end, and I ask that you watch over my career so that my servanthood to others is finished with a blessing. That I do not lose sight of that and that I know the reward is worth the work, and when it is all said and done. I will live a long life happy and reaping the benefits of the work I sewed.

(Father, I pray a special prayer over those who may have already fulfilled their duty to their communities. I pray that they can enjoy the fruit of their labor. That retirement comes with no PTSD, no diseases, no accidents. They may enjoy a joyful retirement with their families in a way that allows them to relax and also pour out any knowledge they have to those willing to receive it. That they find a church to pour their skills into and make good use of their time) In Jesus' name, amen.

28

PRAYER FOR A NEW LIFE

Dear God, I pray that you move in my life. Whether I have been a lifelong believer or whether this is my first leap of faith in you, I ask that you restart my life with you. I pray that I will not be the same from this day on. I pray that people will see a new side of me and my decisions for my life will no longer be the same. I will embark on a new life that walks in alignment with you God. I pray for a life that has a major element of God not only in my work but my personal life which makes me a new person. In Jesus' name amen.

<u>29</u>

PRAYER FOR JOY

Father God, I pray that as I embark on this career, I do not become calloused to this world or the work I do. I know that dealing with other agencies, other coworkers, supervisors and most of all the people we serve takes a lot of us as public servants. However, I know that you can pour out an endless supply of endurance and joy. The bible says laughter is medicine for the heart, and I ask that you surround me with people who will make this job worth it every day because of the joy we share. Allow me to be a joy to others as we work. In Jesus' name, amen.

30

PRAYER TO REPEAT

Dear Father God, I pray as this thirty-day prayer book comes to an end, I ask that you allow me the fortitude to repeat this. This book will have an impact on my life like nothing before and because of that, I know I need to constantly believe these prayers in my heart. I need a constant reflection of why I do this job and to never forget what troubles I may face as I go through it. Lord, I know that a 20, 25 or 30-year career requires more than a 30-day prayer. So, I ask you to allow me to revisit these prayers over the years and to ground myself in your word and a bible believing church. I ask that if I come across a coworker that is struggling with anything these prayers have spoken to, I will have faith and boldness to help them and guide them in a direction that will help them overcome it. In Jesus' name, amen.

INDEX

ABOUT THE AUTHOR

Israel Rodriguez has worked in law enforcement in several capacities while also being a lifelong believer in Christ. His servanthood in ministry has found him serving in several roles around the church from dealing with audio and video to becoming a youth minister. Passion, humor, and care are the most driving qualities and characteristics for Israel. He believes in teaching in such a way that people see things they have never seen before, experience things in ways people never have before, and taking them places they never would have imagined. When Israel is not working in his community as a sports official, videographer, law enforcement officer, or youth minister, he enjoys traveling with his beautiful wife, spending time with family, working out, or eating pizza.